Jeff's Magnet

written by Madge Alley

Contents

Harcourt

Orlando   Boston   Dallas   Chicago   San Diego

www.harcourtschool.com

Jeff has a new magnet.
He wonders if the magnet will
move his cars.

Jeff chooses a car and holds his magnet in front of it. Will the magnet move the car?

The car rolls across the floor to the magnet. The magnet attracts the car, because the car has iron in it.

Jeff chooses another car.

He holds his magnet in front of it.

Will the magnet move this car?

The car does not roll across the floor.
The magnet does not attract the car.
The car does not have iron in it.

Jeff chooses another car.

He holds his magnet in front of it.

Will the magnet move this car?

The car rolls across the floor to the magnet. The magnet attracts the car. Why does the magnet attract this car?

Will the magnet attract a car if he
puts a piece of paper between
the magnet and a car?

Yes! The magnet is strong enough
to attract a car through the paper.
Jeff's idea worked!

Glossary

attract

magnet

Index